MORE THAN
GRAY HAIR AND GLASSES

BY

Alan Fibish

&

Ernie ZumBrunnen

Original cartoons by Zach Johnson

Bookstand Publishing

www.bookstandpublishing.com

Published by
Bookstand Publishing
Morgan Hill, CA 95037
4081_1

ISBN 978-1-61863-774-1

Printed in the United States of America

ACKNOWLEDGEMENTS

You wrote a book and we got the credit. The first copy of *Ordinary People Extraordinary Days* was published early in the spring of 2013, we showed it to you, saw your interest and quadrupled the initial order. You read the book and began to tell us the stories that follow.

First recognition goes to Carole Fibish and Grace Hawes whose advice and counsel was constant. Cartoonist Zach Johnson is recognized for his superb original cartoons. Pictures from the public domain on the internet have helped us tell our stories. Some of you found old photos to tell your story. Willamette View photos come from the corporate and resident web sites.

FOREWORD

We at Willamette View are a varied bunch. When we try to describe a neighbor, we often laugh and say, "you know, gray hair and glasses," knowing that the backgrounds and experiences that led us here from myriad places are the 'more' referred to in the title. We are here and love to tell tales from the past. Some bring forward a story of heroism, some an historical, hysterical moment and all are mixed into this mélange we offer you.

If you are as wise and fortunate as we, and live here, you will find that the stories that emerge over the dinner table are in random order. You are invited to read this book from front to back, or if you wish, to open and read at random, and your random will be just as good as ours, and an approximation of the dinner table random.

The authors have chosen to start with a tale we found amusing. So here we go with book two.

CONTENTS

*Original cartoon by Zach Johnson

1

DONNA KRASNOW

Important Announcement

I taught middle and high school students for 34 years, half of the time in Norwalk, Connecticut, the other half in Carmel, California. Although the towns and student bodies of the two districts were worlds apart, both offered ample opportunities to observe how people (both students and staff) respond to challenges. Most, I would argue, respond with some degree of grace - but not always.

In 1975 I taught 6th grade at Ponus Ridge Middle School in Connecticut. Our principal was new, well, new to us. He had been at another middle school in town for many years and his take-charge/accept-no-nonsense reputation preceded his arrival. We knew we were in for an interesting ride. By the time June rolled around, we thought we knew what to expect. The *Library Incident,* however, changed our minds.

There were, indeed, new things to learn about our principal.

It started innocently. The librarian shared her concern with the principal that students were not retuning their library books. School was soon to close and many books were still missing. Our principal was livid and, as was his wont, he took to the P.A., fury in his voice. It went something like this:

"Attention, attention, attention! I am MOST displeased to hear that many Ponus Ridge students have FAILED to honor their commitment to our school library. Our librarians work VERY HARD for all of you and the LEAST you can do is be responsible and RETURN YOUR BOOKS ON TIME. This is NOT acceptable.

I am going to read the list of students who have yet to return their books. If you hear your name, IMMEDIATELY go to your locker, get the book and march it and yourself down to the library. If you are in 8th grade you will NOT graduate if your books are not returned. I am MOST displeased."

And with that he started reading the librarian's list:

"Alcott, Louisa May

Cleary, Beverly

Hinton, S.E.

L'Engle, Madeline

Lowry, Lois . . ."

As he continued to read the list of authors, we teachers, in our classrooms, were trying to control our laughter. As one familiar name after another was read over the P.A. we wondered when he would finally realize that he was reading from the wrong column of the librarian's list. It took all the way to the Ts, when he hit, "Twain, Mark." that he suddenly stopped and then, in classic Saturday Night Live-style, we heard, "Never mind" and the PA went silent.

3

We never heard another word about those books and we tried to keep a straight face whenever we saw him. It was not easy.

(Co-author's Note: I love this story, but it might well reflect on me as a principal. I figured out early on that the emergency intercom was just that and disabled the device by taking out a key part and hiding it where only a trusted subordinate and I could find it. Else I might have been the fool. AF)

2

SANDRA HELMICK

Easter Bunny

The train passed through Umatilla, Florida (pop. 28) at mid-day -- no, it passed by. There was no crossing, but the whistle blew. Sandra, not yet three, was on the porch of her house on Main Street, the only street, and that is why the whistle blew. She waved and the engineer and conductor waved. Then Sandra would agree to take a nap.

Sandra and her sister searched and found this early photo. How clear it is that she would only take a nap when she was ready!

In the spring of 1943, Sandra was three years old and sick with tonsillitis. Her father, a doctor whose office was next to the house on Main Street did not approve of removing children's tonsils, although he would agree to do so at the request of parents. He also did not immunize his children; he told his wife that if he immunized every other kid in town, he didn't need to treat theirs.

While Sandra was sick, she could not sit on the porch awaiting the train whistle and her greeting from the conductor. But – to everyone's surprise— on the Friday before Easter the train stopped and the conductor brought a three-foot-high stuffed bunny rabbit to the door for her!

Sandra continues, "At least this is what I remembered, and my mother confirmed the story. However, this memory, and many others, was often disputed by my sisters. I acquiesced to their challenge and stopped telling the story as something that really happened. I began to believe it was only a childhood fantasy and mother was no longer around to defend it as true. I moved far beyond that small town and my childhood.

"Fast forward to 2005; my brother is terminally ill. I make the long trip back to Florida to say good-bye to him. While I was at his bedside, a friend from his childhood came to visit him. He said he had not seen me in over sixty years. Then he recalled how he was there at my house when the train stopped and indeed a three-foot-high bunny rabbit was delivered to the door for me.

"I did get that bunny! I can now go back to telling that cherished story."

3

JAMIE MIYATA

Errol Flynn and Relocation

Jamie helped with the housework. If something needed scrubbing, she scrubbed just as hard as an eight year old could scrub. When she had earned thirteen cents, she bought a three cent stamp, wrote a letter to Errol Flynn, Hollywood, California, U.S.A., "Dear Mr. Flynn, please send me your picture," put the letter and a dime in an envelope mailed it and then, impatiently, waited at the mailbox.

Jamie's mother hurried her as the family was being relocated. They were to be taken from their home. Relocated was an euphemism for jail. They had to be because they were Japanese. Technically Jamie was half German-Irish and half Japanese.

General deWitt, sector commander recommended relocation of all Japanese on the West Coast to the

President, saying, "one drop of Japanese blood and you were Japanese." (shades of *Showboat* and that approach to race.) Jamie pondered and said that she was at least 50 drops. Jamie was Japanese, not Irish-German-Japanese and would be relocated. But, not yet, Errol Flynn's letter would not know where she was.

Finally on the day the family was taken from their home the letter arrived containing a first-quality glossy print of Errol Flynn dedicated to Janet Miyata.

Into the midst of the terrible sadness of the relocation, first to Tanforan Race Track, into a horse stall fashioned into a crude bedroom smelling of manure, then to a camp in desolate Topaz, Utah went the Miyatas with the little girl happy to have her photograph.

Jamie brought this treasure with her to Willamette View and has instructed her family that when she dies that the photo be cremated with her and the ashes scattered with her. Jamie laughs as she tells me this, still the resilient little girl who could not be crushed when the events were in fact crushing.

When Jamie finished telling her story, she mentioned that fellow resident Edward Arnold told her he was stationed at Tanforan. The relocation train left Tanforan for Utah as the troops arrived to be encamped in the smelly stalls. They didn't meet then, but seventy years later.

4

CAROLE FIBISH

A Really Big Chocolate Bar

The president of the Sisterhood got pregnant and the vice president assumed her duties. I was the vice president. Now I had to do everything including attending the National Sisterhood convention in San Francisco at the Fairmont Hotel.

The high point of the convention was to be the premier performance of Leonard Bernstein's *Chichester Psalms.* That was special, but if you asked the Fibish children who were then five, seven and nine, their answer would have been the chocolate bar.

Sisterhoods are fundraisers. Fundraising opportunities abounded and the canvas bags were full each night when I came home. There was always a half pound chocolate bar. The kids ran to the door and the winner brought in the bag of loot. The chocolate was reserved as a dessert treat.

Each day when I picked up the bar of chocolate, I filled out a card for the big bar that was to be presented the last day, in the full knowledge that I never win.

The *Chichester Psalms* were breathtaking. I was in the process of buying the recording when friends came to tell that I was being called to the prize table. To my surprise I was given a box the size of a breadboard with a ten pound chocolate bar inside.
When I got home, the chocolate was not in the bag, it wouldn't fit. Earl, the eldest, was able to heft the bar and bring it in.

I remember the Bernstein premier. The kids remember the chocolate.

5

CURT ROBINSON

A Safe Assignment

Curt's infantry unit was ordered to Yakima, Washington for regimental testing. His unit had the top score and they were chosen to remain in Yakima to assist in exercises where Curt's infantry unit was to train providing support to tank units. Yakima was hot and dusty in August and getting the assignment was not seen by the troops as a reward.

Curt got to ride in the tank, a reward for an infantryman. Like the assignment to Yakima, the bumpy ride over rough terrain made walking look like the better option. Then the tank broke down and took two hours to repair. The tank commander informed all that they had to catch up with the rest of the unit and would have to go cross-country. "Get ready for a rough ride."

Infantry support? Curt was atop the turret hanging on for dear life as the tank bumped along at top speed. The ride was finally over, Curt got off first and ribbed the driver, "that was a hell of a ride!" The astonished driver looked at Curt, amazed, gasped, "You could have been killed, you were supposed to be inside the tank!"

Next at Fort Lewis, the unit participated in "Operation Dud", locating and gathering many years' worth of unexploded shells of all sizes. If you found one, you stayed with it until a demolition expert arrived to handle it.

Late in the day Curt found a three foot long artillery shell and sat on it while waiting. He was told by the company commander to set it on end and to catch up with his truck unit, a distance away, and to return to camp for chow. When he stood it up, he noticed that the tip was missing and that the top of the inside was shiny.

He complied with the order to leave, and when he had walked about a hundred yards, there was an explosion. He looked back to see the demolition expert dead!

The Korean action was over. Curt had been assigned to non-combat duty, lucky to be states-side, the safe-side.

6

GRACE HAWES

Autumn Color

Grace was new to Northern California. On a lovely autumn day, entranced by the exquisite beauty of the roadside leaves, she clipped and brought home armloads of fall color. Big, big mistake. Alas, the fall color was poison oak, so virulent that it only reluctantly, and in its own good time, responded to cortisone.

She suffered mightily from her ignorance of the local flora. You will notice she is NOT in the photo of those who uprooted blackberry bushes as a Willamette View Earth Day activity.

7

HILLMAN "LUEDDY" LUEDDEMANN

Air Worthy?

Lueddy enlisted in the United States Air Force. Of course he wanted to be a pilot. He was eighteen: why shouldn't he want to be a pilot? He passed the preliminary evaluation and started his training. Assigned to basic training at Merced, California he began a few days of initiation and then went on his first flight.

The pilot sat in the forward seat and Lueddy in the rear seat of the open cockpit training plane, a Ryan PT. After a few soft turns, the pilot announced on the intercom that he was going to test the passenger for air-worthiness.

The first test maneuver was a tight loop. Lueddy was pressed down into his seat. The next test maneuver was a full snap roll. Lueddy snapped right and left as the plane snapped left and right. Inertia does that.

On the third test maneuver, a slow half roll, the plane is flying upside down. Lueddy dropped from the cockpit. Gravity does that if you haven't fastened your seat belt! This was his first flying experience and no one told him to fasten his seat belt. Inertia and centrifugal force had saved him during the first two tests. It is like swinging a pail of water over your head-- you don't lose a drop. But invert the pail over your head and you can expect to get quite wet.

Fortunately, our young would-be aviator was wearing a parachute. He quickly remembered the instructions on use of a parachute. Landing safely in a farmer's field and un-harnessing from the chute he walked to the nearest farmhouse. The farmer answered the knock on the door and, astonished at what he saw, asked "Where in the world did you come from?" Without uttering a word Lueddy pointed his right index finger straight up.

Back at the air-base, there was a serious hearing on the incident. Fortunately, the pilot appeared and said: "He is just a young kid. It was entirely my fault. I should have checked his seat-belt and I didn't. I accept full blame." The hearing-panel agreed and Lueddy was exonerated and greatly relieved.

He did so well that when he graduated he was assigned to Randolph field in San Antonio, Texas to train as a flight instructor. Later, he was assigned to his old base at Merced. On training flights, instructor Lueddemann *ALWAYS* carefully instructed his students to fasten their seat belts!

8

CARTER BOGGS

CAVU

Carter's father phoned Henry Troh's airport—really airstrip--as it was grass, not paved, and got the report CAVU. Ceiling and Visibility unlimited. He had planned for Carter's first experience in general aviation aircraft. Remember FIRST.

Carter was in love with planes and aviation from an early age, as this picture with his aunt Lorraine shows.

The flight instructor put Carter in the front cockpit of the Piper Cub. Carter knew about all of the instruments and the control stick—his interest in aviation led him to read every bit of information he could find. He knew to belt himself in. (Authors' note to reader—see *Leuddy Ludemann* in this volume.)

Carter continues, "The prop was spun and the engine roared. The takeoff was smooth and uneventful and we climbed to about 3000 feet surveying the countryside. I enjoyed the view as we leveled off and the instructor demonstrated several slow turns to each side. I was encouraged to gently maneuver the stick and airplane. After about 20 minutes the instructor asked "do you like roller coasters?"

"Yes! The airplane was put in a steep climb and just before what I later recognized was a stall, the left-wing dropped and we wound up in a vertical dive with the earth turning in front of our eyes. We were in a spin which lasted 3 full turns. I had seen spins in the movies. The earth really seems to rotate. I was too fascinated for airsickness.

"We proceeded back to the airport where we completed several "touch and goes" before the airplane finally landed. At this point Troh proceeded to berate the instructor in no uncertain terms as he was afraid of scaring off perspective students with stalls and spins particularly on the first flight.

"I continued my flight training within local flight area and particularly with airport traffic pattern practice. Early on, this environment was all visual flight controls without any general radio communication.

"My first dual cross-country was launched from Troh's in early October '56, landing at Springfield and McMinnville and returning to Troh's. My first solo cross-country started at Troh's, proceeded eastbound along the Columbia River and then turning southbound at The Dalles landed at Madras. I got 'lost' only once but quickly identified ground features and essentially stayed on course.

"My first solo cross-country was a triple success. I got to my destination, walked away and the plane was undamaged.

9

DALE HARRIS

Humor In A Somber Setting

I had a few memorable experiences in unexpected places. These two occurred during funeral services while I served the United Methodist Church in Bend, Oregon.

The hardest kind of funeral to conduct is one for a person you did not know. Then you must depend on family members to give you some information about the deceased. In this particular situation the family was from out of town and arrived only shortly before the scheduled beginning of the service. I met with them briefly and was distressed to see that one son was visibly intoxicated. He said "Make r short. Jus say my mother wus a gud wumun. Then si-down."

I must add that the owner of the funeral home, a very accomplished and respected professional, was out of town. The service was in the hands of a newly hired assistant named Charlie. I had barely begun the service when the inebriated family member jumped to his feet and shouted "I said, Jus' say my mudder was a good wumun. Then si down." Charlie, standing behind the family, leapt two feet in the air. The surprised members of the congregation looked shocked and dismayed. I calmly assured him that the service would be short and if he would kindly sit down for the benefit of everyone else then we could proceed. Family members managed to subdue the unruly one, Charlie regained his composure, the congregation relaxed and the service was shortly over.

The second occurred during a committal service just north of Bend. It was a new cemetery with a magnificent view of the Three Sisters Mountains but with no trees yet grown tall enough to shield folks from a bitter wind.

One thing I learned in seminary was that if the family insists on having a fraternal organization involved in the service, make sure it is separate from your part.

In this case I was very glad I had followed that counsel. It was a stormy day with rain coming down horizontally. Only the funeral director and I were wearing long raincoats. Everyone else had on much lighter jackets. I had finished my part of the committal service and invited the designated representative from a fraternal order to do his part. He began in a halting manner to read their ritual and continued by saying, "And now our brother has entered into blessed immorality…" It was really hard to keep a straight face.

10

CARL ILLIG

Bike Ride to San Francisco

Sunday night, June 11, 1939 was special for Carl. For the first time since he was five, there would be no school on Monday morning. Carl looked at his diploma from Benson Polytechnic and smiled. His father, a contractor, spoiled his mood by telling him that he had a job to complete and that Carl was needed.

Mid July and the job was finished. Carl used some of his summer wages and bought a *NewDeparture* two-speed hub for his balloon-tired bike. He installed it, thought about his now state of the art bicycle, called his friend Frank and suggested they go off on an adventure. The World's Fair was in San Francisco and he was in Portland. A seven-hundred mile bike ride? The *NewDeparture* hub said to Carl, "No problem!"

A blanket roll and some clothes and off they went.
Two days in the hot sun rendered Carl dehydrated,
heat exhausted and in a motel to recover.
Reenergized the boys were off, but riding at night,
eating at diners, sometimes taking fruit off of a
roadside tree but riding toward their goal, Carl's
uncle's house in Oakland.

Their budget, diminished by that night in a motel,
was stretched by his uncle's generosity. Three days at
the fair and some time enjoying his cousins' company
came to a sudden end when a playground accident

left Carl with a sprained ankle. There would be no bike ride back to Portland, but a bus ride with his leg up on the seat and the bike with the *NewDeparture* hub under the bus with the luggage.

11

ANNE MCDONALD

The Queen Mother Smiled

Anne searched the room for her friend Helen. It was her second year of teaching at Sellwood school and Helen had been the good friend that helped her to make the last school year successful. Principal Button spoke of his plans for the year but Anne heard only some of them.

Anne went to her kindergarten classroom to prepare for the first day but she could not stop thinking about Helen's absence. At noon she took her lunch bag to the staff room to find that Helen was in England as a Fulbright exchange teacher. At that moment, she saw herself in England teaching there, with her position at Sellwood School filled by a teacher from England.

Anne had taught at Big Lake School in Minnesota before coming to Portland, but that did not count toward her tenure and only permanent teachers were eligible for Fulbrights. She settled in at Sellwood for four years and did so well that Principal Button wrote the perfect letter of recommendation.

Anne was now in Liverpool at the Florence Melly Primary school where she taught for one semester before going to the Fetcham School in Surrey. She taught math and that included the English monetary system which then included crowns, pounds, shillings, pence and farthings.

The Fulbright teachers were invited as a group to Lambeth Castle to meet the Queen Mum, as she was called. The day arrived and it was a perfect Spring day. All had been directed as to protocol: do not talk too much; you are Americans so you need not curtsy; say a few words and let the Queen Mother move on.

The moment came. Anne tried a curtsy. The Queen Mum asked a question which needed an answer, not just a few words. Then she did not move on, she asked another and another and yet another. She then moved on.

Tea and cakes and Cucumber sandwiches were there but Anne's excited state would not let her nibble. The day came to a close. Ann was elated for days—no, years, for the memories of that meeting persist to this day.

12

CAROL CAMERON

A Bad Day?

"Jim's plane has crashed and there are no survivors." A close friend had called to say she just saw the TV news report that Jim's plane had crashed and that all passengers and crew were killed. Carol was devastated.

Jim was an advertising executive with Young and Rubicam working on a presentation for Proctor and Gamble. He was scheduled to meet with their top executives to pitch a new ad campaign. He was in New York at the time and he stopped at his associate's office to pick him up for the flight to P&G's headquarters office in Cincinnati, Ohio.

His associate advised him that the story board wasn't finished. Jim's response communicated disappointment and anger.

"It'll take another hour" was the response. Without

any reasonable alternative, Jim asked his secretary to book them on a later flight. This was Jim's bad day, everything went wrong.

Carol, deeply sorrowed by the news of the plane crash, went from disbelief to joy when Jim phoned her from his hotel in Cincinnati.

He started to explain why he hadn't called earlier but Carol wouldn't let him. She well remembers the day that he missed his plane because he had a bad day.

13

MOLLY BLOOMFIELD

Molly and King

Molly Bloomfield and her family used to spend every summer at her grandfather's farm in Finlay, Ohio. She had two sisters, one seven years old and one ten. The oldest sister, Sue, was crazy about horses and got a beautiful four-year-old Morgan horse that Sue named King. Molly loved it when her sister put her up on King and let her be led around the pastures.

One morning the summer Molly was three, she was playing with dolls in the house yard while her mother hung up the clothes. Her mother went in the house to get another basket of laundry. When she came out, Molly wasn't there. She called but got no answer. She went around the hedge to see if Molly was using the outhouse. Molly was not there. Where was she? Molly knew she was not supposed to go into the farm yard or barn as there were just too many animals and dangerous farm equipment.

Molly's mother began to get worried and she went to find Molly's Dad and they started looking everywhere. Molly's Dad knew how much Molly loved King. Maybe she had gone to his stall to give him a carrot or some oats. When he got to the stall, the door was open and Molly was sitting in the straw between the horse's front legs, picking off the little yellow fly eggs. King's legs and body were covered with flies and he was trembling but he did not move. As soon as Molly's Dad swooped in and pulled her out, King started stamping his legs. No one knew how long she had been there, but what an amazing horse to stay still and protect this little girl.

Molly was punished for disobeying her family and putting herself in danger. She never did that again!

(Authors' note: Molly provided the photo on horseback. We miss her and so wish she were still with us to inspire us with her courage and to share her company.)

14

JOHN GUTENBERGER

Tiger Hunt

A tiger killed a deer. It was close to the village and the townspeople were irate. The neighborhood was in China near the border with Thailand, where John, a missionary's child was born.

The men in his village began to plan a tiger hunt. John really had no choice but to go along. One man had a shotgun and several had muzzle loading rifles. They decided to go to the scene of the deer attack at dusk and climb trees to await the return of the predator.

The time between dusk and darkness was brief in that part of the world. They arrived too late. The tiger had apparently already come and gone. In any event it was nowhere to be seen, so after a short wait they decided to go home.

On the following evening they set out a little earlier.

As they approached their destination they saw the tiger feeding on another deer. He charged toward them and they beat a speedy retreat. Nobody fired a shot. The beast stopped short because it was more interested in finishing its dinner than in attacking the hunters.

This proved to be the end of the grand plan to wreak revenge on the tiger. To this day, John wonders why no shots were fired, but he clearly remembers the day that a tiger was not killed.

15

ALAN FIBISH

Eureka

The prof just finished calling the roll. As the names were called my smile broadened until I could hardly answer "here" when my name was called, but I had answered and was officially enrolled.

It was the summer between my junior and senior years at Cal and I had sat in lecture calls many times. I had never had the sense of discovery and satisfaction that I had that day.

Eureka, I would have said if I were an ancient Greek. I may have muttered, "I've been looking for this course for a long time."

I had survived chemistry, organic chemistry and quantitative chemistry course where I received a chemical unknown which I had to test and describe:

Zoology with sharks to cut up and eggs from which to extract embryos. Many courses with term papers and those in huge lecture halls filled with those who existed only to raise the average.

That day, when the professor called the roll he called my name, many names I did not recognize and 40 others. which I did. As he read the first, I tried to place just why the name was familiar. As he read the second, third and fourth the connection became apparent. When he had read them all, it dawned on me that they were the names of the Cal varsity football team.

Eureka, at last I had found the 'snap' course that I sought in my first three years.

I took ten courses in my senior year, did not hear the name of a football player again and worked much harder. But I had my brief moment of discovery.

16

GLENDA FRENCH

January 27th or $4.54

Glenda appears in Willamette View ads. She can ride a bike a long way. She is willing to make a snow angel. She had a distinguished career. She seems to have it all together. Her story proves that she is not "Super-Woman", but human. Her story in her own words follows:

"I am woman; therefore I usually carry a purse. My purse has my car key and my cell phone which contains all the phone numbers that I no longer have to remember. It has my wallet, thus, all my ID, credit cards, and cash.

"My car 'key' is a fob. When I loaded the car for a trip, I just stuck the fob in a pocket. When I left daughter Medora's house in Seattle I had the car packed with my stuff, all my stuff except for the purse.

"I drove from North Seattle to south Tacoma, about 60 miles, then stopped to get gas. I reached for my purse. I didn't have it. I searched the car. No purse, money, phone, credit cards, phone numbers. The gas station was part of a convenience store. I went inside and there were two employees. They had nothing to say.

"I'm in a fix", I said. I explained the situation and by this time, neither had spoken to me nor altered their expression. Great, I was thinking. People who work in places like this must see all kinds. They seem to be trained to show no expression.

"I am pacing and thinking out loud. Finally, I said to them, "I don't know what to do but call 911." No word to me but he handed me the phone.

"I phoned 911 and started with this is not a life threatening emergency but I left my daughter's home in Seattle and now I am at a gas station in South Tacoma and I left my purse at her house. My car key is a fob that I had in my pocket so that's how I got this far. I have no money, credit card or phone. "Ma'am, I'll connect you with the police, they can help you."

"I explain again, the numbers are in my cell phone and I don't have her phone numbers memorized. The police told me to call 411 and let them get the numbers for me.

"I ask the mute guys for permission to continue using their phone. I got a wide-eyed stare but still no word, no nod, no nothing. I just went on using their phone. 4-1-1!

"What city please?" I actually gave her the correct name and address of Medora and Tony's home but the phone I was using would not make a long-distance call! It was the only phone available to me and it wouldn't make a LD call!!! OK, stay calm, pace around the store some more.

"I could try and plead my story to some of the customers coming in here. All I wanted was about 5 gallons of gas to drive back. Should I beg? I had observed so much of it for a month in India. Did I learn anything? Yes, look at me, diamonds in my ears, Rotary fleece vest on, nice car? Pace and think of another plan.

"I know Maria's home number, maybe I could call it but she never answers and she wouldn't recognize this number I'm calling from. Oh, yea, and this phone won't make a long distance call anyway.

"What about AAA? My card was in my purse! Oh yea! That Toyota Car and Roadside Care package I bought when I bought the car. It was in the glove compartment! I called the 1-800 number and after the explanation, location, waits and holds on the phone I was told that 3 gallons of gas was allowed for roadside assistance. They would send someone out within the hour. "I don't think only 3 gallons will get me back." "I'm sorry but that is all that is allowed." "OK. Let me ask you this. Will I be able to get 3 more if I drive up the road a distance and go through this process again?" "I don't know. I've never had that asked. I suppose you could try but I doubt it would be allowed so close together." OK, just get me the 3 and I'll figure it out from there."

"Please wait while I get the information for you." Another long wait and she comes back and says, (are you ready for this one?) "I'm sorry. They cannot deliver gas to a gas station." Now I am about to lose it. "You're not kidding me are you?" (I'm deliberately trying to stay calm so I can think), "OK look, there is a Denny's parking lot about 12 feet from where I am parked. If I drive there, can he deliver it to Denny's restaurant parking lot?" "Let me check." More waiting on the store phone. "OK it is Auto Rescue and he'll be there within the hour."

"I said out loud to the mute employees, "I'm getting desperate. I'm about to leave you one of my diamond earrings as collateral, if you give me 6 gallons of gas and I'll be back to give you the money and get my earring. (I first thought that one earring would be enough because you couldn't just wear one then remembered guys will wear just one and besides they had no way to test to see if they were just cz or whatever the fake diamond is called). Anyway, it didn't matter they still just stared at me with no physical or verbal response. If they had to learn that in convenience store school, they should have gotten an A plus.

"Then I remembered that last week I had finally memorized Bob's phone number. IF he was home then he could call Medora. I felt excited and out loud said, "I remember a number where I could get some help maybe." Then deflated I said, "but it's a Portland number."

"The senior guy spoke, HE SPOKE! "I'll get my cell phone!" I could have hugged him but refrained. Instead, my eyes filled with tears, "Thank you. I'm getting to the end of my rope."

"Bob answered on the first ring, got Medora on the other line, asked for my location and gave it to Medora. I heard him say, "You gotta step up here and help your Mom." I thought I said, "Don't come now. I have no idea how long it will take to get this gas as they said it could be an hour. I'll drive to wherever I can and beg a phone and call her. Just give me her cell phone number."

"I waited 45 minutes and Auto Rescue showed up. A clean cut big guy with a gas can and a big smile. I said, "I don't think 3 gallons will get me there but I'll be a lot closer." He said, "I only have two and not sure it is even two."

"Is this a joke?" I told him some of the story while he poured his almost 2 gallons into the tank.

"He went back to his truck to get paperwork for me to sign I assumed and came back, held out his hand and said, "This is all I can find but it should help you get another gallon or so." He had three one dollar bills and about 1.54 in change. $4.54. You know me. My eyes filled with tears. He looked like he needed the money. "Will you give me your name or address so I can pay you back?" "Please. Take it and I hope the rest of your evening goes better."

"I drove the few feet back to the gas pump and sat there wondering why in hell (By now I was tired and frustrated and mad) why in hell didn't somebody come to give me the gas. After about a minute, I remembered I was in Washington and had to pump my own. Wondering how you pump and pay with cash, I saw a sign in big letters "Pay Inside First." So I went inside and gave the mute guys $4.54. I got the gas and drove to Tony and Medora's house. I knocked on the door and Tony came and asked, "Where is Medora?" "I don't know. I thought she was waiting here for me to call her." "No, she went to Tacoma to give you your purse!" "But I told her to not come until I called again." He called her on her cell and she started back home. I asked if I could borrow Tony's cell phone, I would meet her as I now had enough gas to get half way back to Tacoma. But Tony's cell phone was out of juice and needed to be charged and--Medora had the charger!

"So I waited until Medora arrived. Bless her heart. She had put in about 6 hours driving that day, first from Vancouver BC. She wondered if it was payback for a fix I'd had to get her out of when she was young but it wasn't. She is a good kid!"

17

ROXANE AND RAYMOND RIVA

How Sweet The Music

Roxane and Ray's stories, although separate, have a unique connection that emerged as we read the two stories. Ray's story first:

When I was studying at the Sorbonne, the choir of the University sang Bach's St Matthew Passion with soloists from the Paris Opera, including tenor Nicolai Gedda. We performed at St. Eustache Cathedral, near Les Halles and the Pompidou Museum of modern art.

And for weeks afterward at the University buildings, as classes changed, in the reverberant stairwells a choir member would begin singing a passage, and others would join in one by one. And gradually the halls themselves seemed to be singing with sound, halls ancient in years, and yet ever young in spirit.

And then, as one by one, the singers left, the music would stop: leaving now the background sounds, sounds merely of voices in multilingual conversation, and of the real, mundane world, recovering-- unwillingly-- from its glimpse of the sublime.

And now Roxane's:

In the 60's, the Chicago Symphony Orchestra had yet to establish its own symphonic choir and regularly engaged instead the concert choir of the University of Illinois. In my Freshman year we joined with the CSO to perform Vaughn Williams' Symphony Antarctica, in which women's voices sing the chill winds blowing cold and death.

The first half of the program, Saint-Saens' Organ Symphony, found us free to wander the basement halls and dressing rooms. Cherishing a piece of plaster fallen from the aging basement ceiling (Orchestra Hall! I was THERE!), I explored the backstage innards of the huge auditorium, wandering more and more Stage Right in a cloud of background music.

Suddenly the orchestra fell silent, and paused.

And the full organ diapason, 64 feet basement to ceiling, opened above me at absolute volume, a multilayered, soul shaking chord. I was under the sound, inside the sound, shaken to the fullness of my being, music filling the hall, the audience, and my soul. I do not remember the rest of the day. .

(Authors' notes: These separate experiences predated their marriage, yet somehow predicted it. The Rivas continue their love of music with the Willamette View Chorus, Ray is in the center of the above photo.)

18

ERNIE ZUMBRUNNEN

Survivor's Tale, as remembered by Ernie ZumBrunnen

I came to amidst a pile of luggage. Was it in a dream that I flew through the air? Obviously not. I was on a train heading for San Francisco to report for basic military training. The train was crowded. Speeding down the west side of the Sierra Nevadas the engine and all of the cars but three had derailed. My photographs are fuzzy but my memory is clear. I can see the cars on their sides, some upside-down, some crushed. Six-thirty on that November morning, I awakened; not everyone did.

Those who were not injured helped people get out of the rail cars, some through broken windows. Dead bodies were then lined up at the side of the tracks and covered with sheets taken from the Pullman cars. At last the railroad people arrived on the scene and from that point forward, we were ordered to touch nothing and to stay out of the way.

Another train had pulled up behind us about a half mile away. Since our efforts were no longer needed, I walked toward that train to determine if that was to be our way out. I could see two enlisted Navy men in uniform heading in my direction from that train. As they came nearer, I recognized both of them. They were Roger Klassy and a pal of his from Wisconsin. I had known both of them back home, where we encountered each other numerous times playing high school sports.

During a visit to Wisconsin recently, I saw Roger again. We agreed that the number of dead was fourteen, the injured about two hundred and all the other details. This in spite of the fact that the railroad company listed the death toll at nine.

I lived through a train wreck. Preparing for war, I escaped death.

19

PAT BURKE

Witness to History

Pat Burke put down the phone and composed herself. That was President Kennedy's secretary on the phone. The president would be at the Burke home at three and it was to be a completely secret meeting, That meant that no one was to know. No one!

What should this 'little Irish lass' serve the President of the United States? The secretary laughed and suggested cheese and crackers and *Coca Cola.*

The Burke home was clean, no, spotless. Pat went from room to room and looked for non-existent dust motes. Cheese and crackers were in the larder but Pat went to the store to buy *Coca Cola.* Husband Walter Burke arrived home about two.

Walter Burke was the President of McDonnell Douglas Astronautics Company, which was to be chosen by NASA to head up the space program at its inception. Burke solved insurmountable problems by dividing them into a set of smaller problems, solving each in turn until the insurmountable was surmounted.

(Pat Burke told one of the authors that when she came to McDonnell Douglas as a secretary, Walter Burke told her that he would marry her! They were married within a year!)

The President arrived, completely in control of the situation and at ease. He found that Pat was Irish born, recognized Walter Burke as Irish as he and just might have nibbled at the cheese and sipped the *Coke*. He quickly got down to business. Pat's memory is clear and she quotes the President, "We must put a man on the moon in this decade and you'll head up the team to do it!" Walter accepted the challenge, the president departed and in Pat's own words. "I collapsed!"

Walter then went into action as the engineer and leader that he was, breaking down the problem into pieces for which there were solutions. In less than seven years, The Eagle landed with Aldrin and Armstrong. Armstrong took that *"one small step"* that made history.

The meeting was brief. The momentous achievement was quickly realized. Pat Burke witnessed a dramatic moment in the history of the exploration of space.

20

LINDA AND CARL MARSCHALL

Goats Of All Sizes

If you live in Penngrove, California and are lucky enough to have both some extra land and a child of 4H age, animals will become part of your life. Erin Marschall, Linda and Carl's daughter, raised goats. That means she milked goats. Then she went to college. Now Linda milked goats, fed the milk to pigs, butchered pigs, sold the young male goats (wethers) to Greek and Indian restaurants, fought off a bear, went to the county fair where she ate a corn dog and risked other dangers.

The Marschalls liked goats, but these goats were just too big. They, in this order: read about Nigerian Dwarf goats; visited Florida and Texas Nigerian Goat ranch breeders; bought a breeding pair in Texas; established Car-Lin Farms, one of the first in the area; stepped back and waited. Soon they had a flock of a dozen. (authors' note: the males are fertile at seven weeks(!) the females can be bred at seven months. They can be bred three times in two years.) It didn't take long to go from two to twelve.

If you raise Nigerian Dwarf goats, you get the *Nigerian Dwarf Journal.* Carl read the *Journal* and found that the Biosphere in Tucson, which was in fact a huge terrarium, about the size of Willamette View, was going to change the livestock in this huge exhibit. He wrote Biosphere. He offered to sell a pair. Car-Lin Farms reputation was such that the deal was consummated.

Now there were not a dozen, but ten.

Car-Lin Bandito was placed in a dog carrier, as was Car-Lin Cara. Big carriers were required as the goats weighed more than sixty pounds each. They took the carriers to the airport, arranged to arrive in the cool of night, met their goats in the baggage area about midnight and looked in vain for the representative from the Biosphere. She wasn't there, only the cleaning crew was. Most of the lights were out. Linda looked at Carl and blamed him for writing the letter that offered the goats. If he hadn't written the letter, they wouldn't be in the cargo area of the Tucson Airport at midnight.

Finally, an airport employee arrived, pushing a flat bed truck. The goats were loaded, pushed out the door where Marschalls and goats met the representative from the Biosphere who despite the alcohol on her breath took charge. The Marschalls went to their Hotel to get a good night's sleep before they toured the Biosphere.

The Marschalls donated a baby goat to a 4H member, reducing the flock to a more manageable size.

That 4H member undoubtedly grew up, went off to college leaving her parents with the goats. Those parents might now be writing stories like this one.

21

ROGER LA RAUS

Impersonator Par Excellance

Most of the time, Roger is not 424 years old, but when he is, Roger is Willamette View's and our nation's oldest resident. Born in Scrooby, England in 1589, he sailed as "Lawfull La Raus" aboard the Mayflower in 1620. He has traveled to every continent on the planet, appeared on the Today Show and NBC TV News and been called "bizarre but effective" by Tom Brokaw.

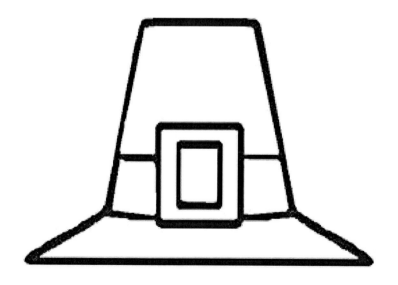

In his most recent fifty year career as a teacher, school administrator and university professor, he has presented the Pilgrim voyage as "Lawfull La Raus" to audiences nation-wide. He has also appeared as "Obadiah La Raus, the last living veteran of the American Revolution" and "General U.S. La Raus, the last living veteran of the Civil War". Returning from the Soviet Union, he spoke as "Col. General Rudolph Alexeyevich La Rausov, Soviet military attaché". He has also presented as "Romulus Lazarus, Roman legionary and the last survivor of Pompeii". After a fellowship in Japan, he reported to American audiences as "Rikimaru Ra Rossitake, vice-president of Global Development for Mishuto Industries of Japan" on the topic "America, the View From Japan: Is Excellence Scrutable?" The Chinese invited him to speak at the Beijing Academy of Educational Sciences, and the Defense Department sent him to Europe where he appeared on Armed Forces TV as Soviet officer La Rausov. Back in America he had to think fast to save his assets from local Evanston, Illinois police.

He was in his Soviet uniform, next to his car in front of an Evanston school, preparing for his presentation to students. As he was inserting the magazine of his Soviet AK-47 assault rifle into the weapon, it kept catching instead of sliding into place.

Comrade La Rausov heard a car door open, followed by footsteps on the road and a voice demanding: "Sir, is that weapon activated?" Turning, he saw an Evanston police officer crouching in the street with his hand on his pistol. Roger waved the empty unattached ammunition magazine at the officer and presented his U. S. Treasury Department permit for the non-fire-able replica weapon. As Roger describes the situation: "Making history come alive is often full of surprises!"

22

JOANN LINDIA

Calabrian Garden, American Pest

Papa and Mamma Lindia, JoAnn's husband's parents, came with their children to the United States from Calabria, Italy. Although they didn't speak English, they opened up a "Mom and Pop" grocery store in Cranston, Rhode Island, selling among many items fresh produce from their newly-planted Italian vegetable garden. They sent their six children to public schools where they learned English, then came home to teach their parents the new language.

The family prospered. Their oldest son, John, earned a doctorate at Harvard and became Deputy Director of Career Education in the U.S. Department of Education in Washington, D.C. It was there in the early 1980s he met and wed JoAnn, the executive secretary of a non-profit organization.

When John retired, he and JoAnn returned to Rhode Island and purchased an old English Tudor house on Narragansett Bay. Shortly after, when Papa came to live with them, he often sat on a folding chair in the back corner of John and JoAnn's yard and, as John would dig up a big clump of weeds and soil, Papa would hit it against his leg, with weeds piling up on one side of his chair and weed-free soil on the other. Whether it was the Rhode Island climate, the care given, or the Italian heritage, the garden rewarded their efforts with tomatoes, eggplants, peppers – hot and sweet – all kinds of squash, and the wonderful smelling basil, oregano, and mint herbs. It blossomed and made Papa seem to be back at home in Calabria, Italy.

The Lindia family enjoyed the harvest, that is, if they could get to it before the woodchucks, raccoons and the occasional deer did. The smaller wild animals had their homes in burrows over the cliff behind the house. Even a tall fence wouldn't keep them away. John purchased a Have-a-Heart trap that would trap but not harm the animals, baited the trap with surplus vegetables, and placed it near the garden. When a woodchuck or a raccoon was trapped, animal trap and all were taken to the countryside and the animal released.

JoAnn once went to the garden, and to her dismay, found a skunk sleeping in the trap. After a brief discussion with John and the flip of a coin, JoAnn lost and returned to the trap, quietly opening the trap door, then returning to the house. Later that day, they found the trap empty, the skunk somewhere else, and a collective sigh breathed. After that, John and JoAnn decided not to trap any more animals, and shared the garden with their "four-legged friends".

23

HELEN CONWELL, M. D.

Stone Age Meets 20th Century

A Motilone warrior shorter than his five foot long arrows, lay on his back, braced his bow with his feet and sent arrow after arrow in the direction of the oil crew. This was the greeting sent when anthropologists, government agents, oil companies and missionaries, came to the jungle.

Although the warrior was physically small, his notched arrows could do great damage or kill. The arrow shafts were multiply notched in both directions, and usually when a victim was struck, well intended "rescuers" actually hastened death by trying to pull out the arrows, which then caused fatal bleeding.

The Motilones were a vicious indigenous tribe, living deep in the interior near the border with Colombia, one-hundred miles from Maracaibo, the center of the oil industry and the place where Helen and her husband lived.

Every attempt by anthropologists, government agents, oil companies and missionaries to approach the tribe was met with a barrage of arrows. Theirs was a stone-age culture, a real anachronism in the middle of the twentieth century.

The exploration company's cook started his day building a fire, and was struck in the upper body by two of the arrows. The arrows protruded from his body about six inches in front and about four feet in back. None of the crew tried to pull out the notched arrows but cut them off flush with the skin, both front and back. They loaded him into a pick-up truck and sped to the surgical hospital in Maracaibo. He was fortunate because in the city there was an excellent thoracic surgeon, U. S trained Dr. Gustavo Garcia Galindo.

Helen started the anesthesia. One of the arrows had penetrated his liver, and the other one had gone through the right lobe of the lung. Helen says the conduct of the anesthesia was uneventful but that she had to fend off a throng of people in order to maintain contact with the patient. It seems The National Surgical Congress was having their convention in town and understandably, they all wanted a close look, so pushed their way into the small operating room.

When she made rounds the next day and asked how the patient was feeling, his only complaint was: "Doctora, hay muchos mosquitos". There were no screens on the windows. Mosquito bites seemed to be a minor inconvenience compared to the experience he had just had-- as probably the first human to survive a Motilone attack.

Helen concludes: "I have always enjoyed recalling this experience, savoring my being a participant in the abrupt meeting of a primitive culture with the (relatively) advanced one we offered that day". She also tells us that in 1961, eight years later, a lone nineteen-year old missionary from Minnesota named Bruce Olson, representing the outside world, finally made peaceful contact with the tribe.

Professionally, Helen was an anesthesiologist. Her singling out this incident from a long and rewarding professional career and her observations on the juxtaposition of modern and stone-age cultures let us see this life-saving event through her eyes.

24

SOLON STONE

Klamath Forest Protective Association

During World War II there were few men to do the jobs that needed to be done, so the Klamath Forest Protective Association hired high school boys for the work. At age 15 you could get a work permit and fight forest fires. My first experience was on a fire north of Klamath Falls, after school, at night, with little training. The pay was 65 cents an hour. I thought it was GREAT!

In April I went to the KFPA office to get on their list for a summer fire protection job. They provided training on several Saturdays--how to use the tools for fire fighting (shovel, axe, polaski, hazel hoe, water can, crosscut saw)--how to build a trail around a fire--how to read maps and find your way in the forests--how lookouts find fires and tell fire crews where they are. This was a nice, practical addition to my sophomore year in high school.

Classes are over and I'm off to my first full-time job. The truck took us to the Penny Springs camp--25 miles west of Klamath Falls towards Ashland on the Green Springs highway. A cook house, the boss's cabin, cook's quarters, shower house, AND

TWO SQUAD TENTS. That's it! Beautiful! Hey, room and board plus $100 per month, twelve days on two off, who can complain?

A fire crew is 4 or 5 guys. The crew chief is someone who worked here last year. At 16 or 17 he is experienced. He has done many fires, knows the roads in the area, and can get the other jobs done.

During May and June the roads have to be cleared of fallen trees big rocks and boulders so that you can get to fires and do other work. Many of the roads are old railroad grades used when the region was logged by rail. This is when you develop your skills with the axe, crosscut saw, cant hook and peavey.

The crew chief drives the pickup. By the end of the summer he's a good mountain road driver. Iron wire telephone lines get knocked down. They are put in trees using telephone wire and porcelain insulators. Oh, another skill is required. Climbing trees using tree spurs and belt like a telephone or power lineman. We once had to move nineteen miles of line.

In June, July, and August there are fires, most caused by lightning. Almost all are small because the lookouts on mountain peaks spot the smoke and direct a crew to the fire after locating it on a map. They stay up all night when necessary to keep a log of lightning strikes. If smoke is seen the next day the lookouts can triangulate the location.

There is always work to be done. Felling a dead fir tree is a good source of firewood and bark for the office in town. Pry the bark off using a steel bar or just cut it off with an axe after a section is cut off using a crosscut saw.   It's really good exercise. Down on your knees pulling that saw thru the log-usually in the hot sun. But, the skills a high school kid learns are all valuable when it comes to fire fighting.

What is a fire? Well, it might be in burning brush and ground trash. The top of a tree hit by lighting is another good spot for a fire. Fell the tree, make certain the fellers don't get hit by limbs falling from the tree.

Put out burning or hot material using dirt and dust; water is not usually available. Use your hands to make certain the fire is OUT.

Should the fire be bigger than a spot fire, build a trail around it using polaskis (a combination of an axe blade and narrow hoe blade), hazel hoes, shovels etc. Bulldozers and other machinery are not usually available unless the fire gets big.

School starts. Your Penny Springs job is over. Its back to classes unless the town people can't handle the fall fires. At that time you may get called to fight fires.

That's the first year with the KFPA. Summer comes, I've finished my junior year. I am now16, and it's back to Penny Springs. I am now a crew chief! The pay is the same $100.00 per month, BUT I drive the pickup!

Now, please tell me why would anyone put a 16 year-old in charge of three or four other 15 or 16 year olds and let him drive a pickup in the woods to fight forest fires? He picked me and it all worked out with me as the crew chief.

25

CAROL STEEN

Terror In The Night

Frightened? Of course Carol was frightened. A large man neared, jabbed her in the back—was it a gun or his fist? His arm was around her waist now and he was hitting her in the back.

She had grown up on a farm and came to Portland to work as a secretary to the branch manager of the First National Bank of Oregon. She was on her way to a hotel meeting of the Eastside Commercial Club, an association of young businesswomen. Young businesswomen dressed appropriately, hat and gloves, stockings and dress shoes.

The meeting turned out to be much longer than she planned so she decided to leave before it ended. The city was quite small in those days. She had walked one of the two blocks to the bus-stop when the assailant grabbed her.

She broke free and ran from the shadows to the middle of the street. Suddenly a young man in Army Uniform arrived on the scene. He had seen the man following Carol. He yelled, "Get the hell out of here" at the bad guy, who immediately fled the scene.

The soldier further proved himself by accompanying Carol to her bus stop and remaining with her until her bus arrived. Although she says she subsequently had a number of unusual experiences, she states with a pronounced degree of certainty: "this one was my most unforgettable!"

She wonders to this day who the soldier was and wishes she could thank him again!

26

BOB THOMAS

A Bicycle Ride in Beijing

I made my first visit to China in the fall of 1985, my luggage had been sent to Minneapolis! I was a Professor at Wayne State University who, along with a small group of U.S. and European scientists, had been invited by Professor Shuyi Zhang and the Institute of Acoustics at Nanjing University. That year was just at the beginning of 28 years of economic growth for China at an average of 9.7% per year, and my impression of the enormous population of Shanghai and Nanjing was that everyone was dressed in gray – as they had all been during the Mao era.

Flying into Shanghai at night for the first time was a very strange sight for a westerner used to looking down at the arrangement of street lights along big-city streets and highways, seen from the air. Most of the lights to be seen were from a random array of charcoal cookers!

Riding the government car into Shanghai from the airport the scene was dimly lit along the city streets, but teeming with people: cars and trucks in the inside lanes, bicycles in the next lane (much wider than Portland's bicycle lanes), and pedestrians in the outside lane. At every intersection, all of these groups managed to merge and emerge (more or less) unscathed, to continue on their paths. This was quite a scary sight for my sore Detroit eyes! Throughout that visit to Shanghai, Nanjing, and Hongzhou I was fascinated by these traffic experiences. There were no private cars to speak of in those days, and even much of the commercial delivery took place by some form of bicycle. A common sight was a tricycle, loaded down with several pieces of furniture – which I have ever since referred to as Art Van Shanghai Delivery (Art Van is the major furniture chain in the Detroit area). It was just amazing how one person could provide the necessary "horsepower"!

To the Chinese residents of Shanghai/Nanjing, I was viewed as being equally strange. China had been closed to the outside world for most, if not all of their lives, and their curiosity was such that they couldn't resist peeking in the restaurant window to have a look. Many of them were beginning to try their luck at the English language – using the BBC radio broadcasts, and I represented a convenient opportunity to practice. Walking in the park, they would come by to say hello, and when I tried my Berlitz Tape version: "Ni hao", we became immediate friends – great fun.

On my third trip to China in 1992, together with my good friend and colleague, Skip Favro of Wayne State, we had an opportunity to visit the Beijing Zoo, and to have a look at the famous Giant Pandas. As we stood in front of the Panda exhibit, we suddenly realized that all of the Chinese visitors to the same exhibit were watching the two Detroiters more than they were the Pandas! During this trip, we were hosted by the Chinese Academy of Sciences, and housed in a hotel that they used in northwest Beijing – not too far from the several Institutes and Universities that we were visiting. Also working at one of the Institutes then was Ms. Xiaoyan Han, who was to join our research group as a Ph.D. student later that year. The hotel had bicycles for rent, so Xioayan, Skip and I decided to spend a day of sightseeing and shopping in central Beijing, and to travel there by bicycle. These bicycles were standard Beijing type – nothing fancy, but always equipped with a little bell on the handlebar, operated by the thumb of the rider – presumably to alert the several hundred strong throng of vehicles, bikes, and pedestrians traveling along with us on our journey.

The pace for a bicycle ride in Beijing was very different (much slower) than that in Portland, as was the attire. Riders dressed as they would for work – so it was common to see women in dresses and heels, and when it rained, they managed it by using very simple, functional ponchos. With the streets packed with bicyclists, a pretty uniform pace was the norm, with the pack moving together. It was illegal to carry a passenger on one's bike, but it was also quite commonly done – with the passenger disembarking (temporarily) if the intersection was supervised by a policeman. With cars, trucks, bicycles, and pedestrians all flowing together in an intersection, the slow pace allowed for a huge game of chicken, with horns (and for us, our little bicycle bells) warning others to give way. The trick was to act as though you were totally unaware of every other vehicle, but move slowly enough so as to minimize the damage if you lost the game of chicken. Somehow we succeeded for the hour or two that it took us to reach the center of Beijing, where we parked our bikes along with hundreds of others.

Xiaoyan led Skip and me on a very interesting walk in the Hutong – an area of old Beijing where people lived geographically in the way residents had lived for centuries – in sections adjoining very narrow alleys. She asked the two of us if we would like to see the inside of one of these, then went in and inquired of the resident (an elderly man) if he would be willing to invite the two Americans to have a look around. Not only did he agree, but as it was noon, and he was preparing dumplings for lunch in his one-room home, he invited us to join him. We had a bit more exploring to do, and a long bike ride back before dark, so we politely declined, but his hospitality and the kindness and hospitality of almost everyone whom we met made a deep impression on me. As for Xiaoyan, she came to Wayne State University, received her Ph.D. in Physics, and currently is leading her own research group as a tenured full Professor of Electrical and Computing Engineering. She, and her husband Chunlin Liu, and her son Hans remain among our most cherished friends to this day.

27

ARDEN JEWELL

A Walk to School

"You saved my dad's life." The stranger grasped my hands, pulled me from my chair and hugged me. I was bewildered and embarrassed. Had he confused me with someone else?

It was at my Grant High twenty-year reunion. I had not really felt the need to attend as I was a student at Grant only for my senior year and did not feel a deep connection to the class of 1949. My parents had moved from a small town in Idaho to Portland when my dad was appointed pastor of the Rose City Park United Methodist Church.

Fortunately there was a large youth group and it was easy for me to become part of a new circle of friends. Often a group would meet on the corner of 58th and Alameda to walk twenty blocks to school, saving our bus fare so that we could celebrate after school and buy a *Yaw*s hamburger and a cherry coke, my favorite!

As the stranger continued his story my memories resurfaced.

I stood on the corner waiting for my friends and saw a man lying in the street, near the curb. It was damp and foggy and although there was not much traffic that early, the cars that sped by came too close to the body and I realized that he might be run over.

I knew that I could not move him to safety so I flagged the next car and asked the driver to protect him while I sought help. The corner drug store across the intersection was not yet open but I could see there were lights on.

I pounded on the door and screamed for help. The owner finally opened the door. He called for an ambulance and I raced back across the street to help divert traffic. The ambulance came, my friends arrived and we walked to school, knowing that the drunk had been taken to jail or the hospital, the excitement faded and was forgotten.

Twenty years later I learned that the man I assumed was a drunk was in fact a prominent businessman who had suffered a heart attack and was close to death as he lay in the street.

I walked to school that morning thinking that I had saved money for a hamburger; years later I found that I had also saved a life.

28

PHIL MIRKES

Amateur Rocketry

Phil developed an early interest in rocket science. He and a young friend read an article in Popular Mechanics and decided to build a rocket. They found an aluminum tube of the appropriate size and proceeded to accumulate the other necessary ingredients.

The eager pair met in Phil's backyard on the agreed-upon testing day. It was a Monday and his Mom's weekly wash was hung on the clotheslines to dry. The "newbie rocketeers" loaded the fuel, placed the rocket in the shiny tube and lit the fuse. An amazing volume of flame was produced, but the rocket didn't move any more than an inch or so.

It didn't take a proverbial rocket scientist to determine the cause of the problem--insufficient fuel. A substantially larger amount of fuel was added and the second countdown commenced. Voila! The rocket emerged from the aluminum tube and slowly climbed to an altitude of approximately five feet where it disintegrated in a catastrophic explosion.

Neighbors came running from all directions to determine the source of the mighty blast. What they observed were hanging sheets, towels and items of underwear, almost all of which bore telltale holes and scorch marks of various sizes. Phil tells us: "To put it mildly, Mom was not pleased!" A noble experiment was thus abandoned and Phil changed his primary interest to a less violent undertaking that has served him well.

29

ALAN NYMAN

New Home Room Teacher

Washington High in San Francisco is less than two miles from the Pacific Ocean. "It's damp and it's foggy said the home-room teacher and I won't return to Washington, I'll teach in the warm Mission District where I won't wheeze so much and you'll have a new home-room teacher."

A new home-room teacher for our senior year! It was obvious to his home-room that they had driven the others out and they waited to intimidate whomever they were assigned as a new home-room teacher.

The new home-room teacher arrived, just out of college, equipped with youth, large size and the wisdom imparted to all brand new teachers, "Don't smile until Christmas."

Others in the class readied for the contest and Alan Nyman shrunk deeper behind his desk unready for any battle. The new teacher was his brother-in-law, Alan Fibish, and any misbehavior would be reported directly to his mother. So A. Nyman behaved and feigned ignorance of any relationship. A. Fibish also feigned ignorance and over dinner at the Nyman home garnered from A. Nyman bits of information that would allow him to control this what might have been a fractious class.

Thus did Alan Nyman survive his senior year with satisfactory deportment grades in home room and Alan Fibish survive his first year of teaching with absolutely no discipline problems in his home-room class.

Alan Nyman, his older sister Carole, still married to Alan Fibish, and Alan Fibish are Willamette View neighbors each of whom will attest to the veracity of this narrative.

30

GENE SEIDEL

Change in Itinerary

"I'm Sorry, Mr. Seidel, your flight from O'Hare to Indianapolis has been cancelled, tornado warnings! There is a commuter flight from Meigs Field that has two seats available. You can get there by taxi in time to make the flight."

Gene and a colleague had to be in Indianapolis to conduct a seminar the next morning. They took the cab and arrived at Meigs just in time to board the flight and be told that there were just two seats left on the 21-seat commuter plane. "One of you will have to sit in the co-pilot's seat. Will that be OK?"

Gene looked at his partner and sensed his panic. So Gene took the co-pilot's seat and strapped himself in. He would be able to see the storm more clearly than the other twenty-one passengers who would be able to see little through the small side windows.

Gene's and the pilot's seats could be seen by all of the passengers. There was no door or curtain separating them. All of the events that were to transpire added to the anxieties of the passengers.

The plane taxied to its position at the end (start?) of the runway where takeoff was delayed. The weather was bad. Anticipating that it might take a while, the pilot pointed to number of things that Gene should not touch as well as the fire extinguisher under his seat that should be used if needed. He then lit a cigarette, it was 1969 and it was permitted.

Cleared for take off, the plane flew into the storm. The weather worsened over Lake Michigan. All the passengers could see the pilot's struggles to control the plane. Suddenly the pilot yelled to Gene, "Grab the fire extinguisher under your seat and put out the flames between us." Gene remembered the pilot's cigarette but said nothing. Gene and the pilot extricated the extinguisher and put out the fire.

When the tower was informed they were ordered back to Meigs. There they were met with emergency vehicles. Passengers were unloaded and left to make alternate plans.

Gene and his partner managed to get to Indianapolis but that is another story.

31

TOM McALLISTER

The Hunt That Lasted A Lifetime

Steens Mountain in 1970 is where I shared a lifetime hunt with my sons. The youngest of our trio, Michael, 15, drew a once-in-a-lifetime Oregon bighorn ram tag. Scott, 17, and I were support team, spotters and packers.

But first, the event that made this hunt possible— restoration of the California or Rimrock Bighorn which had vanished from Oregon. The last few were seen in 1912 on Hart Mountain. These bighorns inhabited semi-arid intermountain ranges between the Desert and Rocky Mountain races of bighorn sheep.

Competition with vast bands of free-ranged domestic sheep that carried diseases to which wild sheep had no immunity and unrestricted hunting brought rapid extinction for the Rimrock Bighorns.

At the time it seemed such a small, uncertain

beginning when 20 bighorns leapt from a stock truck driven 36-hours straight through from Canada. They were released by Coleman lantern light in the wee morning hours of Nov. 8, 1954, into a 34-acre pen at the base of Hart Mountain

I was there as The Oregon Journal outdoor editor to report on this historic reintroduction. The Oregon Game Commission (now Oregon Fish & Wildlife Dept.) had been invited by the British Columbia Game Department to receive surplus Rimrock Bighorns trapped from the last known bands at the northern extremity of their range, the dry interior side of the Coast Range near Williams Lake.

On their arrival in Oregon a 600-acre holding pasture encompassing Juniper Canyon on the west face of Hart Mountain was completed. Any bobcat, cougar or coyote in the vicinity had been trapped in advance. The 4 1/2-mile protective fence was eight-foot high woven wire with buried barbed wire strands to prevent coyotes digging under.

Those bighorns prospered. Releases from this natural holding pasture soon stocked that area, and then transplants began to Steens Mountain in 1961, the Owyhee Breaks in 1965 and onward through their historic ranges including the lower John Day and Deschutes canyon country. In ensuing years Rocky Mountain Bighorn were also restored to historic ranges in Oregon's Wallowa and Blue mountains and Hells Canyon,

The reintroduction of native fauna was the essence of this program. I never imagined when participating in the release of those initial 20 Rimrock Bighorns that a son of mine would hunt a trophy ram in Oregon. But Michael, who was born in 1955, drew one of six tags issued for a 1970 Steens Mountain hunt. Scott and I in the ensuing years applied for but never drew a bighorn tag. So, we relive our once-in-a-lifetime experience with Michael on the face of that 30-mile rip in the earth's surface, the Steens fault block thrust 5,000 feet above Alvord Desert.

From the summit rim at 9,000 feet elevation the

mountain dips gradually westward while the eastern face plunges. In the Pleistocene Period the upper third of this eastern scarp was glacier scalloped into U-shaped basins that spill into V-shaped stream clefts surrounded by cliffs topped by erosion domes and intersected by vertical dikes. At the run out onto Alvord Desert are boulder covered alluvial fans. It's a perfect mix of all-season range, escape and shelter for bighorns.

Weeks before his hunt Michael and a schoolmate backpacked into and scouted this bighorn domain. Days later they hitched a ride from Mann Lake Ranch with a Nevada cattle buyer to Burns where they called home. It was Big Alvord Creek that Mike chose for his hunt.

His reason for the bottom up approach was the certainty we had of an easier and safer return. Coming off the top rim of the Steens is treacherous, and it's easy to get rimmed-in.

As it turned out we had the advantage of being able

to glass upwards into the basins and under the soaring rims. We could also catch early morning sheep movement down slope to day bedding areas.

The day before the hunt we climbed ultra light with our pack boards from Alvord Desert into a keyhole where Big Alvord Creek plunged over a rock face. By picking out a game trail we worked high above this gorge and by evening were on a sliver of terrace just below the alpine cirque.

We spread sleeping bags (no tent). Michael dropped down to the creek and filled canteens by flashlight while Scott and I used a split boulder face in the lee of the mountain downdraft for our fire.

We arose as Orion The Hunter faded in the dawn. We climbed onto the north ridge to glass and minutely examine the great cirque, for the entire morning if necessary, to spot that one trophy ram. Less time stalking around and more time sitting and observing is the way to bighorn success.

My lifetime hunting partner, Jim Peterson, Beaverton

druggist who had West Slope Pharmacy, sent his 20-power spotting scope with us. Scott latched onto five rams with it.

They were lined out on a game trail indented into loose talus. It angled down from the headwall of the cirque toward what we correctly assumed would be their day beds on the ridge across from us.

Rather than all three make a move we told Mike he was on his own. The lad went to live that hunting adventure of a lifetime over the next two hours. The rifle was his dad's carbine, a .308 Finnish Sako with Mannlicher stock.

Through a frosty dawn Scott and I stayed on our perch, looked down on this overpowering stage set and then soaked in the warmth of the rising sun. From our eagle perch we watched Michael cross Big Alvord, climb to pick up the game trail and follow it through a saddle with a mountain mahogany stand where the five rams, followed by three more, passed from sight. At 10:43 a.m. we heard one muffled shot beyond the opposite ridge and headed there.

When Scott and I crossed that south ridge saddle a bedded full-curl ram erupted from those mahoganies. Michael's tracks were impressed onto those of the rams. They led us around the base of a soaring eroded lava dome. In its east face was a long cleft or chimney and it enclosed a still shaken Michael beside his massive ram. Mature rams, at 7 to 8 years, run more than 300 pounds. This one had horns broomed on the ends from combat and wear.

Michael's hand trembled as he signed his tag and related a hair breadth encounter with three great rams. "Man, I'm telling you I was out of my mind when those things came at me," was the actual quote his reporter dad wrote on the back of Michael's Dear Sportsman letter from the State Game Director. The letter was authorization for the six hunters who drew Steens tags to take a three-quarter curl or better ram Sept. 26 through October 1.

I still have that letter. Those field notes were penned after locating Michael in that chimney where he first heard rocks rolling. It was some 25 feet wide at that point. A single ram looked down on Michael from atop a rock the size of a Chevy suburban. Two more rams came down the chimney onto the rock where they paused together. "I had the pick of the century. Three rams stood in a little circle 50 feet above me. I was shaking so I'd have missed if it had been any farther," reported Michael.

With one shot the ram he picked toppled and lay at his feet. The other two either had to come right through our hunter or go upward into a cul-de-sac.

"I thought they'd knock me off when I shot, but one ram went back up that chute like a locomotive hauling dust. The other sprang to a ledge above me. Then he jumped 15 feet into space. I'd unloaded the rifle for safety right after dropping my ram, but now I was trying to reload. I thought they would come right through me."

That's exactly what happened. The rams had no way out and Michael was in full defense mode with rocks spilling down to be followed, he knew, by the rams. He said when they came hell bent in his direction it was seconds to impact. He put the rifle down and pressed himself against the chimney wall. He could feel the wind from the motion of the hurtling rams.

"I was never so shook in my life, my body was tense and I was shaking so I was doing that rain dance. I was scared shitless." And that's when an event from his favorite sixth grade book flashed into his mind. It was The Black Wolf of Savage River, A Story of the Alaska Wild, by Ernestine Byrd, 1959, Parnassus Press.

This story of the black wolf from pup to alpha pack leader has a chapter, Adventure in the Crags, in which a couple of Dall Sheep rams charge the young wolf and try to butt him off the crags. Body pressed to the chimney wall. That was Michael's flashback.

Before the day faded we'd skinned a full shoulder cape for a taxidermy mount and boned out and packed Michael's once-in-a-lifetime bighorn ram off the upheaval face of Steens Mountain.

32

WINNIE THOMAS

African Adventure

Winnie reflects on a harrowing incident in Africa in 1970, maybe 71. The incident is clear, the date not.

"I was living with my husband and 4 children in what was then Rhodesia (now Zimbabwe). Our oldest two children, Paul and Mary, were attending the Waterford School in Swaziland. Waterford was a non-racial boarding school, with an international reputation. Nelson Mandela's two daughters were also attending that school. The son of Seretsi Khama, the leader of Botswana went there. Anyway, Paul and Mary wanted to be there so they wouldn't be forced to go to an all white high school in Rhodesia. Several other missionary families from different denominations sent their kids there for the same reason. We parents took turns driving; it was my turn, so our minibus was FULL of kids headed back to school. My job was to see that they all got there safely and on time.

"Shortly after we crossed the border (and the Limpopo River) into the little town of Messina (now Musina), and then about 20 miles up a hill out of town, there was a tremendous grinding sound of metal on pavement. As ever the alert kid, Paul looked out the back window, saw sparks flying like a trail behind the van. He threw himself over the middle seats to reach past me (the driver) and turn off the ignition switch. Finally the vehicle lurched to a stop, and we all piled out and stood, just gawking -- the engine lay on the pavement, hanging by one bolt, still hot!

"As people do in very rural and foreign areas, the first car coming toward us stopped, assessed our dilemma, and said he knew there was a garage in Messina -- he would have them send us a tow truck. I can't remember exactly, this was a Friday; no way the garage owner could get parts from Johannesburg until Monday. Kids were due at school on Sunday. No train Saturday to Jo-burg. No money for a hotel (probably no hotel, actually), so the garage owner, who lived in small apartment above the garage, said we could sleep in his apartment, then hitchhike to Jo-burg the next day. We broke into smaller groups and went to the petrol station to beg rides to the big city, several hours away. I told all the children to get a ride to the train station, and we would meet there, in Johannesburg. The kids got on a train going east to Mbabane in Swaziland. I called the school to alert them, and then went with my younger son Bruce (who had come along to keep me company on the return trip) to a decent hotel. Oh, my - we treated ourselves to room service! Early Monday morning we caught the train going north to Messina. By the time we got there, and waited all afternoon, the car was fixed. (Chewing gum and baling wire?) We set out for our home in Salisbury (now Harare) with just enough cash left to buy gas. So, no stopping for food. Just drive, until we pulled into our home about 4:00 am. Quite an adventure when you consider life without credit cards or cell phones.

"One of the miracles of the trip was how Bruce, about 7 years old, could keep talking to me so that I wouldn't get too sleepy. He was super, but not super-human, so eventually he did go to sleep, and I was on my own. I think angels kept me awake."

33

ROBERT C.A. MOORE

Finding My Ax

I was taking a noon walk across campus during my sophomore year when a friend stopped me and asked if I was going to the Pete Seeger program that afternoon at the student union. Drawing on my vast well of sophistication, I asked naively, "Who is Pete Seeger?"

My friend looked at me like I had suddenly grown extra eyes and proceeded to enlighten me in ways I could not understand, much less appreciate.
"Just go," she said finally. I went.

There were more people in the auditorium than I expected. Knowing nothing about Pete Seeger, I assumed no one else would either. Being unsophisticated is actually a life strategy that has served me well over the years. I advanced that point of view that afternoon by not really listening to the introduction we were given.

Instead, I fixed my attention and eyes on a foot thick alder log that was positioned, complete with ax, center right on the stage. Chain-saw wood carving was more than a decade off, but this was Oregon, after all, and it seemed believable to me that Mr. Seeger might be about to serenade us somehow with an ax-log combination.

Instead, he came onto the stage in work clothes carrying a stringed instrument I'd never seen before, but quickly recognized when he played.

It was a five stringed banjo and I had to stand up to be sure there were not two people playing it. Luckily, I was able to sit down after less than a half-hour. I was completely out of breath.

I can't remember the whole concert, but I do recall him singing, "Acres of Clams," and "Stagolee."

Then, most of the way through the concert, he put down the banjo and picked up the ax. He sang a work song while the ax accompanied him on the log.

Burl Ives led us to understand that there was a class of songs – folk songs-- of uncertain lineage that would be interesting, pleasing and easy to sing.

That afternoon Pete Seeger instructed me that there is a class of people – namely, everyone – who create and perform music in order to remake the world.

Since that afternoon, I've taken to thinking of myself as a folk song singer (working on jazz now). I thanked Burl Ives and said goodbye to him. I had bought my first guitar a little more than a year earlier on a Korea hilltop. It was an ungainly instrument with heavy gauge strings set on an unhappy wooden box and was capable of making truly awful sounds. I loved it.

Two of the several guitars I have are unbelievably beautiful to look at and play. And I've sung while using an ax on tree parts.

I'm sure I would otherwise have discovered all of this on my own, but I'm still grateful to my long ago friend for telling me to go hear Pete Seeger that day.

34

HUGH HAVEN

The Big Bear Quake

The 1992 Big Bear, California earthquake shook at 08:05 am on June 28. It registered 6.5 on the Richter scale. The earthquake occurred at a relatively shallow depth of 3.1 miles and caused landslides in the San Bernardino Mountains.

This earthquake occurred three hours after the 7.3 magnitude Landers earthquake, which was centered 22 miles to the east. The closely timed occurrence of these earthquakes is an often-cited example of a regional earthquake sequence. Both earthquakes had occurred significantly close to the southern portion of the San Andreas Fault, and the Landers event probably reduced the compressional stress in that area. The epicenter of the later quake was five miles SE of Big Bear Lake.

That morning, my wife Terry and I were visiting friends in Olympia, Washington and we didn't learn of the quakes until later that morning. We immediately called home. Janet, our daughter, was sitting the house and our pets in Seal Beach, California. She said she felt the quake and the aftershocks. She and the house were OK but the streets were awash with water sloshing out of the neighborhood swimming pools. We also phoned a friend in Camp Angelus where our cabin is located. He reported that the quake really jolted him. The epicenter was only six miles away from our cabins. He and his cabin were OK but a lot of chimneys were down and he said that he could not walk across the room without holding on because the aftershocks were so intense. The three hundred homes in Angelus Oaks were isolated. Slides closed Highway 38 on either side of town and later the phones went out and the power was off briefly. The only way in or out was via the Lower Control Road, a very rugged road through the mountains that was only useable by short wheelbase, high clearance vehicles.

Without phones Ham radio was the only way to communicate with the outside. The two Hams in town were extremely busy.

Two weeks later, when all was back to normal the residents of Angelus Oaks determined to do something. They bought and installed ten cargo containers behind the Fire Station, and filled all but one of them with food and emergency supplies. The other one became the Amateur Radio Shack. They called for Amateur Radio Operators and set up a class to train more. I saw the notice in the Post Office and joined the class. We met every Thursday night for twelve weeks. On the following Thursday three radio amateur Volunteer Examiners came to give us the exam for our Technician licenses. The examiners told us the names of the ten who passed. In two weeks the FCC sent us our licenses with our call signs; mine is KF6AOK.

(Authors' note: Hugh continues his interest in Ham radio. Here he is, fourth from the left as a member of the WV radio club.)

35

IRMA DELSON CANAN

'Twas a Gift to Be Simple

In the late 1960s I dropped out of college (University of California at Berkeley) in order to have experiences that felt more 'real' and less abstract/theoretical. I took a Greyhound bus across the country from my home in San Francisco all the way to Boston. I picked up jobs in exchange for housing and meals, and through the capriciousness of life, ended up doing such things as nannying for Rockefellers and serving as companion and caregiver to one of the last surviving Shakers.

Part of my adventure included working for a Quaker family in exchange for room and board. They lived along a beautiful rural road in Canterbury, New Hampshire, just up the hill from the Shaker village. I was fascinated by the Shakers and one day summoned the courage to walk over to their community to introduce myself and make their acquaintance. Over time, of the six remaining Shaker "Sisters" I became friends with three of them: Bertha, Lillian, and Marguerite. They invited me to join them for meals or to have tea and to chat. I began visiting them every afternoon upon completion of my chores with my Quaker hosts. Several months after I began my daily visits, Sister Marguerite, who actually was the Eldress of the community, began to experience failing health and needed supportive care.

She and the other Sisters preferred to remain in their community rather than leave and go into Concord to a nursing home. They asked me to meet with them and told me that if I were willing to move in with Marguerite and tend to her needs she would be able to remain with them. She had developed heart trouble and was becoming "senile." Marguerite was frail and prickly, but she liked and trusted me. I moved in with her in the Spring of 1968. My role was to assure and reassure her that she was safe and not alone, to make sure she ate properly and took her medications, and to keep the other Sisters apprised of her state.

We got on well, Marguerite and I. We had daily conversations; she was curious about my life in the world beyond the Shaker village and I was curious about her life as a Shaker. Marguerite recounted to me the history of the Canterbury Shaker community during her leadership so I could record it in one of the the large, leather bound volumes that told their story since its founding in the late 1700s. Each entry was in the hand of either the Eldress or the Elder of the community setting down the story of the community during their oversight. When it was time for Marguerite to tell her story, she was no longer able to write legibly due to a palsy that had set in. So, she asked me to be her scribe. It was a thrill to hear the story from her and to record it for others to read.

Our days together were generally low key. Marguerite's house was one of the original Shaker houses of the Canterbury Shaker community which had been 3,000 acres in its heyday. The house in which Marguerite and I lived had once served as the community infirmary. It was well suited to her needs, and I loved living within those handcrafted walls and among the furnishings that were designed and made by Shaker brothers hundreds of years earlier. My room had tall, multi-paned windows that still had in them the original glass. Each little rectangle gently distorted the bucolic scene outside; the glass had become wavy with the passage of time. The distortions lent an ethereal quality to the atmosphere. There was, however, one rather jarring note. In this little island of historic and visual tranquility, there was a substantial disruption: in spite of the authentic, original Shaker surroundings and furnishings (which already were much sought after by museums and collectors), Marguerite had purchased an oversized, avocado green, naugahyde recliner that she used exclusively and that she would not allow anyone else to use.

Marguerite was the youngest of five children, an unexpected "surprise" for which her parents were unprepared. They took her to the Shaker Village from their home in Marblehead, Massachusetts, and dropped her off to be reared by the Shaker Sisters. That was the last she saw of them. Even at the end of her life, she spoke of it as if it had taken place yesterday. Unlike Sister Bertha and Sister Lillian whom I also got to know during that time, Sister Marguerite was generally stern of demeanor, prickly of personality, and somewhat reclusive. She had a very spinsterly bearing. The pain of abandonment she wore close to the skin.

One of the most memorable experiences I had with Sister Marguerite was when, together, she and I watched the 1968 Chicago convention on her television, she sitting in her naugahyde recliner and I in an authentic, antique Shaker chair. She was in her seventies and I was twenty-one. We were of different ages, stages, and life experiences. Although we were watching the same images on the same screen in the same room, we saw very different things. She saw unkempt communists and anarchists. I saw idealists speaking truth to power. She found the Chicago Seven repulsive. I knew some of them. The irony of the scene was not lost on me. Sister Marguerite was enamored of her olive green naugahyde recliner and repulsed by the activists. I was in awe of the Shaker furnishings amidst which I found myself and was personally acquainted with some of the convention disruptors. Even at the time, it all seemed topsy-turvy, the way each of us integrated the old and the new in such different ways from one another.

In spite of it all, we had a special appreciation of, and affection for, each other. Now, as I approach my seventies, I think I understand Sister Marguerite better than I did then and have a clearer sense of why things appeared so differently to each of us. In 1987, I returned to the community during a trip to the east coast. By then, the Canterbury Shaker community had transformed from being a dwindling Shaker village to being a museum and historic site, complete with restaurant and bed and breakfast. There was one Sister remaining, Sister Bertha, to whom I had always felt closest. She had become completely blind in the intervening nearly two decades. When I saw her, I greeted her with, "Hello, Bertha!" to which she replied, "Irma, is that you?" It was a poignant reunion and confirmed for me that the connectedness I felt with them was reciprocated. Their history is remarkable, as are their inventions, architecture, carpentry, crafts, agriculture, cuisine, music, and general ingenuity. Their faith was as deep as was their integrity. They were a remarkable people. And, how incredibly fortunate and grateful I am that the capriciousness of fate placed us together for a brief time.

36

CARLA HARRIS

A Life-Changing Adventure

In 1954, I finished my sophomore year at Willamette University early to join ten other students and a professor on a three-month "Europe on a shoestring" trip. Planning had been underway for a year.

We left Salem, Oregon in two ancient Buicks that we had bought for a total of $375. We drove non-stop (except to eat and for "pit stops") to Chicago, where we spent two nights with the parents of one of the students. We sold the oldest Buick and arranged to drive a new car to a dealership in Maine. Our next destination was Quebec City, where we would board the Arosa Kulm, a German ship under Panamanian registry because of that country's minimum operating regulations. Each summer this modest vessel carried American students east and European students home after a year of study in the United States. It would then return with refugees escaping to Canada.

The trip to Le Havre, France took nine days. En route we watched the Queen Mary glide past us heading east. A few days later we saw her returning to America. Most of our group got seasick, but I was spared. Editing the daily newsletter kept me pretty busy. It was put out by a staff of college journalists from around the country. The product was printed on a cranky Italian mimeograph machine and spread the news of daily onboard activities.

When we landed we immediately sought out our order of twelve export-model three-speed English bikes that would carry us through seven countries. The bicycles had been ordered by a member of our group who worked part-time in a bike shop. We loaded them on a train to Paris and began our peddling from that great city.

Our plan was to travel at our own speed, meeting at each new village. The first day out was sunny, warm and beautiful. Traffic was no problem because the primary mode of transportation for the French of that time was the motor scooter. The exception was in

Paris where cars were apparently propelled by honking horns!

We quickly spread out along a lovely country road, with our professor and two or three students in the lead. I followed my friend, Lorraine, who was about a block ahead. There was a group of male students behind us. As the temperature rose, the breeze felt wonderful as we basked in the sunshine and enjoyed the quaint countryside. How could it have been any lovelier? We had cultivated fields, tree-lined roads and an altogether peaceful setting.

After mid-day I became a little dreamy, thinking "I can ride without holding onto the handlebars, like I used to do many years ago". The next thing I knew, I awoke to find myself lying on the road, surrounded by five Frenchmen. I tried, unsuccessfully, to locate my glasses. Pain shot up my arm as I touched my forehead with a hand which quickly became soaked in blood. I began to talk but quickly realized that my little French audience did not comprehend my language. My French vocabulary was limited to a few helpful phrases I had learned on the ship, such as "student from America" and "bad boy".

Suddenly I remembered "porte lunettes" and again felt around for my glasses. One of the men retrieved them for me. I put them on and could see that my bike was now in the bed of a truck. I pointed down the road from where I had come, trying to explain that students from America were behind me. The men were patient at first, and somehow let me know that they wished to take me to a doctor. I declined, emphasizing that my friends would come soon. I couldn't understand why they had not already arrived since they were not far behind me.

Time crept by but no cyclists appeared. Finally the spokesman for the men was able to make me understand that I had to go with him. Reluctantly, I got into the truck, hoping he was an honorable gentleman, and we drove off. "This is something I won't be writing home about" was my thought as we rode along. Unaccustomed as I was to getting into a vehicle with a man I didn't know, I was understandably concerned.

Finally we reached the outskirts of a village. I spotted the rest of my group. Imagine what my professor must have thought; it's only the first day of cycling and here is one bloody female biker riding in a truck with a male stranger.

The fellow students behind me had taken a wrong turn and ended up in the village via an alternate route. One of them, fluent in French, learned my story by talking with my driver, and had been persuaded to deliver me to the village doctor. My bloody forehead was quickly patched up, and x-rays of my arm showed that it was not broken. But because of the sprained condition he advised me not to ride a bike for three days. The visit was free, complements of socialized medicine.

What do I do now? Not riding for three days was unplanned. We looked at train schedules and found that they would be of no help. I insisted that I could ride with one hand-- and I did. Our bicycle expert, who had ordered the bikes, thoughtfully offered to ride along with me the next day to be sure I stayed upright, and that I would have no further sunstrokes.

The rest of the summer was uneventfully wonderful. We biked more than a thousand miles, going seventy-two miles on our longest day. We went as far south as Florence, Italy and as far north as Edinburgh, Scotland. We sold our bikes in Scotland and returned to London by train for our last week before boarding the Arosa Kulm for the voyage back to New York.

On the following Valentine's Day, our bike expert, Dale Harris and I announced our engagement. We were married the following August, and now, fifty-nine years later, still happily are.

37

HARVEY LEFF

Hot August Wedding

August 17, 1958 was a typically hot, humid August day in Chicago. It was the day of the wedding of Ellen Wine and Harvey Leff. The wedding planning had been thorough and despite the expected nervousness of the bride and groom, everything seemed to be under control. The wedding venue was Chicago's Belmont Hotel, where the male and female members of the wedding party each had a hotel room in which they changed into their formal attire.

When Harvey retrieved his tuxedo's hanger, he was surprised to find that although the white jacket was there, the pants were not! Horrified, he mentally traced the recent history of the pants. He realized that when he and Ellen went to a photographer's studio several days earlier to have wedding photos taken, only the jacket was needed. He recalled that he had put the pants on a separate hanger before taking the jacket to the photographer. Unfortunately, upon his return home, he had failed to recombine the jacket and pants on a single hanger, and then completely forgot that they were separated. When he removed the jacket from his closet on the wedding day, he assumed (incorrectly) that the pants were on the same hanger.

It was only an hour before the wedding was to begin that Harvey realized that the pants were at his home rather than at the hotel, where he needed them. Given the time crunch, Ellen's brother Gordon agreed to drive back to the house to retrieve the pants and he left immediately. The wedding party waited nervously for Gordon's return, and to break the ice during this tense period, the men began telling jokes. Harvey's father Jack, who was always quick with a joke said, "Harvey, I know you've been awaiting this day for five years and are extremely anxious, but you <u>do</u> have to wear pants!" There was plenty of laughter and Harvey never forgot that great quip.

After about 45 minutes, Gordon returned with the tuxedo pants and Harvey put them on immediately. Now things were expected to proceed more normally. Because it was over 90 degrees outside and the air conditioning in 1958 was less effective than it is in 2013, the men decided to not put their tuxedo jackets on until the very last minute. As Lohengrin's Wedding March began, Harvey placed his left arm in one sleeve, but when he tried to do the same with the right arm, he found that his right arm would not fit through the sleeve!

He had fractured his right wrist six weeks earlier while playing baseball and was still wearing the original cast. Although he had successfully put the jacket on for the photo-shoot several days earlier, on the next day he had a thin new layer of plaster placed on the cast, which had become dirty and unsightly. So now the cast looked clean, but surprisingly, the slight additional thickness of the new plaster prevented him from putting on the jacket. He pondered what to do as Lohengrin's Wedding March played on.

Harvey envisaged walking down the isle in his shirt sleeves even though that would destroy the formal look of the wedding. Out of the blue, Ellen's mother Rachel said, "Wait a minute, I'll get my sewing kit." She quickly retrieved her purse, where she kept the kit. She took out a small scissors and proceeded to cut open the tuxedo's right sleeve. Being an accomplished seamstress, Rachel was remarkably swift. She soon had Harvey slip his arm through the open sleeve, and while the Wedding March continued, she sewed the sleeve back together. Her speed and efficiency were amazing and her cool demeanor helped to calm Harvey. When she finished, a startled Harvey had the jacket on and the sleeve looked normal.

Once Harvey had <u>both</u> the tuxedo pants and jacket on, the wedding proceeded without a hitch. That was more than 55 years ago, and the marriage has gone smoothly ever since. Harvey and Ellen think it will last.

38

MAXINE NELSON

The War Effort

Maxi graduated from Oregon City High School class of 1943. She had taken a course where she learned skills like riveting sheet metal. Soon after graduation she applied for a job at Community Iron Works, prepared by her course work for the work place.

Hired as a welding assistant she set out to prove that she was a good worker and learner. Soon, the boss approached her to ask if she would like to become a journeyman welder. Her reply, an enthusiastic yes! In the age of 'Rosie the Riveter,' she became 'Maxi the Welder.'

The demands for the armaments of war led many women to work in the war industries. This was seen as a patriotic duty. Maxi was one of these essential workers.

The contributions of American women to the war effort were recognized by posters such as this one.

Small aircraft carriers helped win the war. Maxi, skilled welder, welded sheets that became the hulls of these ships. Thank you, Maxi!

39

MOLLY AND IRMA

Coincidence?

Molly Bloomfield and Irma Canan have been friends for forty years. They were residents of Corvallis. Molly and her family owned a lovely beach house in Waldport on the Oregon coast where, when Irma visited this story revealed itself.

Molly was the chair of the Corvallis School Board in 1994. She attended the National School Boards Association conference in New Orleans. As it was her first visit, she wanted to bring home a souvenir for her husband. While exploring storefront art galleries, she came across one with many small paintings hanging on a fence in an alley. One caught Molly's eye. It was of a chair sitting in a garden. She fell in love with it, made the purchase and took it home to Waldport and hung it in the bathroom.

For over two decades, it hung in the same spot. In

2006, Molly offered the gift of a weekend in the house to Irma Delson and Pat Canan who were celebrating their first anniversary. They drove to the house, unloaded the car, and prepared to relax. There was food in the fridge and wood in the fireplace and they settled in for a mini vacation.

Molly and her late husband Stef were avid art collectors, and their coast house was filled with original works that they had picked up during their frequent travels. "Pat, drop what you're doing and come in here" Irma shouted as she tried to remain calm. Pat followed her excited voice into the bathroom. The suggestion of urgency in her voice was not lost on him. "Look at this painting" she said. "What about it?" he replied. "Look at the name of the artist" she said in a restrained voice. She felt as though she would explode, and wondered if she had gone nuts and might be seeing things. "That's my name! It must have been my father" Irma surmised, her voice filled with wonderment. But how could that be? Why didn't Molly mention this to me?" she asked of no one in particular. Irma immediately phoned Molly and left a breathless and confusedly worded message on the answering machine, asking to be phoned back as soon as possible.

The next morning after what seemed to be an interminably long night, the phone rang and Molly's cheerful voice innocently asked "what's up?" "Molly, you know that little painting in the bathroom, the one with the empty chair sitting in the garden?" "Sure-- that's one of my favorite paintings--why?" responded Molly. "Did you notice the name of the artist?" inquired Irma. "You know, I don't think I ever did. Who is it?" "I'm pretty sure it is my father" was Irma's excited response. "What?--you're kidding--are you sure?" "Well, I'm not positive but I can't imagine who else it could be. My sister-in-law was an artist but it doesn't look like anything I ever saw of her work. I think it was done by my father. What do you know about it? Where did you get it? -- And when?" Molly then described the details of her trip to New

Orleans, how she spotted this little painting and fell in love with it, who knows why. She felt she absolutely needed to have it. Previously, she and Stef had only purchased art when they were together. Making this unilateral decision represented quite a departure from the norm. But she liked it far too much to leave it behind. It grabbed her and wouldn't let go. But she knew nothing about the painting, and in the more than twenty years she had owned it, she had never noticed the name of the artist.

Irma's father was an artist, associated with the Chicago Art Institute and the Art Student League at Pratt Institute. He was Art Commissioner for the State of Florida and designed the Illinois Pavilion at the 1934 World's Fair in Chicago. He was a painter, an illustrator, a sculptor, an architect and a teacher. He died in his forties and the last time Irma had seen him was when she was nine months old. She had no memory of him, no sense of him-- nothing. His presence in her life was through his artwork and stories about him. Believing she was in the presence of a piece of canvas that he had touched and transformed into a compelling garden scene, resulted in an extremely emotional upheaval within her. Pat understood that he had entered the invisible world of Irma's efforts to "know" her father.

By this time, Irma was trembling, and eager to pursue some sleuthing on her own. She proceeded to phone a cousin. A somewhat awkward, but wonderfully informative conversation ensued. "I've come across a small painting that I think was done by my father and it is signed. A friend of mine, Molly Bloomfield stumbled across it in New Orleans. I'm trying to find out if it is his. Do you have any idea of how my father's painting could have found its way to New Orleans?" A long silence followed the inquiry. Irma was familiar with long silences--they typically preceded the revealing of a family secret. Irma braced herself. The answer came: "When your aunt passed away in Chicago, her son discovered a trunk, full of your father's paintings. I asked that he pass some of them on to you, but he wanted to take care of her possessions in the most expeditious way possible. That apparently included shipping the entire trunk to a gallery owner he knew in New Orleans. I'm truly sorry you never got any of that art and we never told you. I'm as certain as I can be that the painting is from that trunk. It is amazing that it found its way to Oregon and to your eyes!" "By the way," Irma's cousin continued, "the Molly Bloomfield you mentioned--Is she by any chance related to Richard and Laura Bloomfield?" "Yes, they are her sister and brother-in-law. How do you know them?" "We knew one another when we were colleagues and friends in a California town"

Irma's next phone call was to Molly. She shook while she was dialing and continued as Molly answered. "It's my father's work! My cousin just explained to me how it got to New Orleans. And guess what? He and his wife know Richard and Laura." Irma and Pat had decided that they would ask if Molly would sell them the painting, so Irma took the opportunity to ask. The reply came immediately: "It's your wedding gift; I insist!" So the painting of the little empty chair in the little garden now hangs on a little wall, a very special little wall in Pat's and Irma's apartment, just one floor below Molly's, who was able to see it there.

40

TWO WHO CAME BEFORE

When we asked Eleanor Crick for a story, she modestly directed us to an article written by Rolla about Colonel Harold Davenport, who lived here until the age of 102. Gifted photographer and newsman Rolla had seen the world from East to West and from pole to pole, but the tale that follows was what he chose to remember.

Davenport was still in his thirties when a horse platoon was added to the battalion he commanded in Berlin in January, 1950. The unit was charged with the care, training and use of some of the Lipizzaner stallions General George S. Patton rescued from Nazi Germany during the closing days of World War II.

These magnificent horses have entertained the public with their graceful ballet-like maneuvers. They have appeared before audiences throughout the world, even in Portland! A lucky few have seen them in the Spanish Riding School Arena in Vienna, Austria, with its white and gilt enhancing the crystal chandeliers.

Col. Davenport was Commanding Officer, 759th Military Service battalion, at the time the horse unit became part of his unit. He and his staff did a marvelous job and it wasn't long before the unit became a "sharp looking outfit." His First Sergeant was a Non-Commissioned Officer in the cavalry, and his experience with horses was vital to the success of the operations.

The future Colonel was born in San Francisco in 1904, weighing only four pounds. After the 1906 earthquake, the family moved to Berkeley where he later graduated from high school. He went on to college and became a teacher and later a school principal. He was a reserve officer when the United States entered World War II. He was summoned to active duty as an infantry officer and assigned to Military Police. He saw active duty in China and was in Berlin at the time of the Berlin Wall. There was intense conflict there, at that time, but Davenport recalled, "Those were wonderful days." His former platoon turned out to be the last designated horse unit in the U.S. Army.

(The authors met Rolla Crick and Harold Davenport when we came to Willamette View. They brought 'more than gray hair and glasses' with them. Their experiences enriched our environment as do the experiences of each of our residents.)

ABOUT THE AUTHORS

We live in a delightful retirement community, Willamette View, in Portland, Oregon, which you can visit digitally http://www.willametteview.org or in person. We hope that you decide as we did that this is a great place to live. If you do, we know that you have a story that we can include in our sequel.

The incidents we describe are told over the dinner table or in the – literally -- hundreds of clubs, resident led, which fill our hours. This book filled our hours, brought us a smile and we hope it amuses you while it tells you about us.

Alan Fibish is a native San Franciscan and a retired high school principal. Ernie ZumBrunnen is a native of Wisconsin and was a certified public accountant.

Zach Johnson has created cartoons to fit our narrative. Zach is a student and is working on his illustrated novel.

CPSIA information can be obtained at www.ICGtesting.com
Printed in the USA
BVOW04s1456070414

349764BV00004B/8/P